# A song of Praise

BIBLE CHAPTERS
FOR KIDS

# Let's tell the world about God's greatness!

"Make a joyful noise unto the Lord, all ye lands."

(verse 1)

Be happy in all that you do for God.

"Serve the
Lord with
gladness:"

(verse 2a)

# Let's sing a cheerful song to Him.

"Come before His presence with singing."

(verse 2b)

# Remember that He is the true God.

"Know ye that the Lord He is God:"

(verse 3a)

# He made us and the whole universe.

"It is He that hath made us,"

(verse 3b)

# We belong to Him, and He cares for us.

"And not we ourselves;
we are His people, and the
sheep of His pasture."

(verse 3c)

Let's keep
God in our lives
with a thankful
heart.

"Enter into His gates
with thanksgiving,"

(verse 4a)

And be grateful when we talk with Him.

"And into His courts with praise:"

(verse 4b)

# Thank Him and worship Him for everything He has done.

"Be thankful unto Him, and bless His name."

(verse 4c)

# The Lord is awesome and deserves our praise.

"For the Lord is good;"

(verse 5a)

# He will always love us.

"His mercy is everlasting;"

(verse 5b)

# And His promises last forever.

"And His truth endureth to all generations."

(verse 5c)

Lord, Your name is great and wonderful all over the earth!

Psalm 8:1
(Paraphrased)

I thank You, Lord.
You are so good,
and Your love
lasts forever.

Psalm 118:1
(Paraphrased)

It's amazing how You made me. Thank You for Your wonderful work.

Psalm 139:14
(Paraphrased)

# More books in the series:

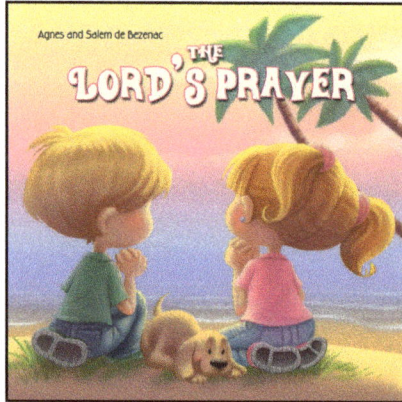

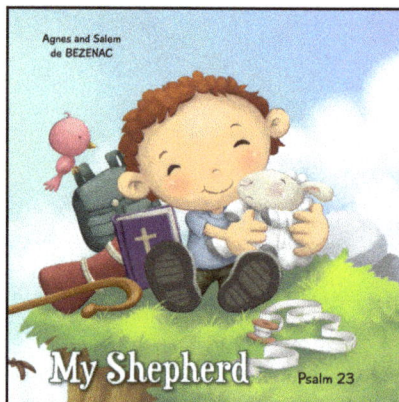

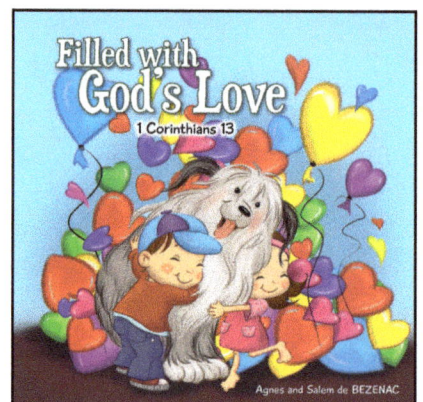

**Agnes and Salem de Bezenac**
THE LORD'S PRAYER

PSALM 119
**Agnes and Salem DE BEZENAC**

**Agnes and Salem de BEZENAC**
SAFE WITH GOD
Psalm 91

PROVERBS

**Agnes and Salem de BEZENAC**
My Shepherd
Psalm 23

Filled with God's Love
1 Corinthians 13
**Agnes and Salem de BEZENAC**

## iCHARACTER

Published by iCharacter Ltd. (Ireland)
www.icharacter.org
By Agnes and Salem de Bezenac
Illustrated by Agnes de Bezenac
Colored by Henny Y.
Copyright 2012. All rights reserved.
All Bible verses adapted from the KJV.

www.ingramcontent.com/pod-product-compliance
Lightning Source LLC
Chambersburg PA
CBHW040250100426
42811CB00011B/1215